WOOD PELLET GRILL
BEEF RECIPES

The Ultimate Smoker Cookbook with Tasty recipes to
Enjoy with your family and Friends

James Stone

Copyright © 2021 by James Stone

TABLE OF CONTENTS

The South Barbacoa

Preparation Time: 15 minutes

Cooking Time: 3 hours

Servings: 10

Ingredients:

- 1 and ½ teaspoon pepper
- 1 tablespoon dried oregano
- 1 and ½ teaspoon cayenne pepper
- 1 and ½ teaspoon chili powder
- 1 and ½ teaspoon garlic powder
- 1 teaspoon ground cumin
- 1 teaspoon salt
- 3 pounds' boneless beef chuck roast

Directions:

1. Add dampened hickory wood to your smoker and preheat to 200 degrees Fahrenheit
2. Take a small bowl and add oregano, cayenne pepper, black pepper, garlic powder, chili powder, cumin, salt, and seasoned salt
3. Mix well
4. Dip the chuck roast into your mixing bowl and rub the spice mix all over
5. Transfer the meat to your smoker and smoker for one and a ½ hours

6. Make sure to turn the meat after every 30 minutes; if you see less smoke formation, add more Pellets after every 30 minutes as well

7. Once the beef shows a dark red color with darkened edges, transfer the meat to a roasting pan and seal it tightly with an aluminum foil

8. Preheat your oven to 325 degrees Fahrenheit

9. Transfer the meat to your oven and bake for one and a ½ hours more

10. Shred the meat using two forks and serve!

Korean Beef Rib Eye

Preparation Time: 10 minutes

Cooking Time: 15 minutes

Servings: 6

Ingredients:

- ½ cup of soy sauce
- ¼ cup scallions, chopped
- 2 tablespoons garlic, minced
- 2 tablespoons Korean chili paste
- 1 tablespoon honey
- 2 teaspoons ground ginger
- 2 teaspoons onion powder
- 2 boneless rib-eye steaks, 8-12 ounces
- Smoked coleslaw
- 12 flour tortillas

Directions:

1. Preheat your smoker to 200 degrees Fahrenheit with peach or pearwood
2. Take a small bowl and whisk in soy sauce, garlic, scallion, honey, ginger, onion powder, and mix to make the paste
3. Spread the paste on both sides of the steak
4. Transfer the steak to your smoker and smoke for 15 minutes per pound

5. Remove the steak when the internal temperature reaches 115 degrees Fahrenheit

6. Cut the steak into strips and serve with coleslaw wrapped in tortillas

7. Enjoy!

Reverse Seared Flank Steak

Preparation Time: 10 minutes

Cooking Time: 20 minutes

Servings: 2

Ingredients:

- 3 lb. flank steaks
- 1 tbsp. salt
- 1/2 tbsp. onion powder
- 1/4 tbsp. garlic powder
- 1/2 black pepper, coarsely ground

Directions:

1. Preheat the Traeger to 2250F.
2. All the ingredients in a bowl and mix well.
3. Add the steaks and rub them generously with the rub mixture.
4. Place the steak on the grill and close the lid. Let cook until its internal temperature is 100F under your desired temperature. 1150F for rare, 1250F for the medium rear, and 1350F for medium.
5. Wrap the steak with foil and raise the grill temperature to high.
6. Place back the steak and grill for 3 minutes on each side.
7. Pat with butter and serve when hot.

Nutrition:

- Calories 112, Total fat 5g,
- Saturated fat 2g, Total carbs 1g,
- Net carbs 1g Protein 16g, Sodium 737mg

Corned Beef with Cabbage

Preparation Time: 20 minutes

Cooking Time: 5 hours

Servings: 6 - 8

Ingredients:

- 1 Cabbage head, chopped into wedges
- 1 lb. Potatoes
- 2 cups halved Carrots
- 2 tbsp. Dill, chopped
- ¼ tsp. of Garlic salt
- ½ cup unsalted butter
- 1 can Beer (12 oz.)
- 4 cups Chicken Stock
- 3 - 5 lbs. (1 piece) Beef Brisket, corned

Directions:

1. Preheat the grill to reach 180F.
2. Rinse the meat and use paper towels to pat dry and place on the grate. Smoke for 2 hours.
3. Increase the temperature, 325F with the lid closed.
4. Transfer the brisket to a pan for roasting. Sprinkle with seasoning. Pour the beer and stock in the pan.

5. Cover with foil tightly and let it cook for 2 ½ hours.

6. Remove the foil and add the potatoes and carrots. Season with garlic salt and add butter slices.

7. Cover with foil again. Cook 20 minutes. Add the cabbage, recover, and cook for an additional 20 minutes.

8. Serve garnished with chopped dill and enjoy.

Beer Beef

Preparation Time: 15 minutes

Cooking Time: 7 hours

Servings: 8 - 12

Ingredients:

- 1 Beef Brisket 9 - 12 lbs. the fat outside trimmed
- 5 garlic cloves, smashed
- 1 Onion, sliced
- 5 tbsp. of Pickling Spice
- 1 tbsp. of curing salt for each lb. of meat
- ½ cup of Brown sugar
- 1 ½ cups Salt
- 3x12 oz. Dark beer
- 3 quarts Water, cold
- Rib seasoning

Directions:

1. In a stockpot, combine the curing salt, brown sugar, salt, beer, and water. Stir until well dissolved and add the garlic, onion, and pickling spice --place in the fridge.

2. Add the meat to the brine but make sure that it is submerged completely. Brine for 2 - 4 days. Stir

once every day and rinse the brisket under cold water. Sprinkle with rib seasoning.

3. Preheat the grill to 250F.
4. Cook the brisket for 4 to 5 hours. The inside temperature should be 160F.
5. Wrap the meat in a foil (double layer) and add water (1 ½ cup). Place it back on the grill and let it cook for 3 to 4 hours until it reaches 204F internal temperature.
6. Set aside and let it sit for 30 min. Crave into thin pieces and serve. Enjoy!

Italian Beef Sandwich

Preparation and Cooking Time: 3 hours and 20 minutes

Serving Size: 8

Ingredients:

- 4 lb. beef roast
- Dry steak rub
- Salt and pepper to taste
- 4 cloves garlic, minced
- 6 cups beef broth
- 8 hoagie rolls, sliced
- 6 slices Swiss cheese
- 1 cup pickled vegetables, chopped

Directions:

1. Preheat your wood pellet grill to 450 degrees F. Close the lid for 15 minutes and sprinkle all-beef roast sides with steak rub, salt, and pepper.

2. Make several slits on the roast and insert the garlic cloves in the slits and grill the roast for 30 minutes.

3. Turn and grill for another 30 minutes and transfer the roast to a Dutch oven.

4. Pour in the broth and cover with foil and place it back on the grill. Reduce temperature to 300 degrees F.

5. Cook for 4 hours, shred the roast, and put the shredded meat back in the Dutch oven.

6. Stir with the cooking liquid.

7. Add the shredded meat and cheese slices to the hoagie rolls and put on the grill for 10 minutes.

8. Sprinkle with the pickled vegetables and serve.

Grilled Steak with Creamy Greens

Preparation and Cooking Time: 45 minutes

Serving Size: 6

Ingredients:

- 2 porterhouse steaks
- Salt and pepper to taste
- 2 tablespoons butter
- 1 shallot, chopped
- 2 cloves garlic, minced
- 1 cup heavy cream
- Pinch ground nutmeg
- 4 tablespoons butter
- 3 lb. mixed salad greens

Directions:

1. Sprinkle both sides of the steak with salt and pepper.
2. Preheat your wood pellet grill to 225 degrees F for 15 minutes, and add the steaks for 45 minutes.
3. Take the steaks out of the grill and increase the temperature to 500 degrees F.
4. Close the lid for 15 minutes. Put the steaks back to the grill.
5. Cook for 5 minutes per side.

6. Take the steaks out of the grill and let rest for 5 minutes.

7. Add the butter to a pan over medium heat and cook the shallots and garlic for 5 minutes, stirring often.

8. Stir in the cream and reduce heat and simmer for 10 minutes.

9. Season with the salt and nutmeg and transfer to a food processor.

10. Pulse until smooth and add the remaining butter to the pan.

11. Stir in the greens and cook for 5 minutes.

12. Pour in the cream mixture and simmer for 5 minutes.

13. Serve the steaks with the creamy greens.

Garlic Fillet Mignon

Preparation and Cooking Time: 30 minutes

Serving Size: 4

Ingredients:

- 4 filet mignon steaks
- 1 teaspoon garlic salt
- Salt and pepper to taste
- 1 tablespoon Dijon mustard
- 1 cup Parmesan cheese
- 2 cloves garlic, minced

Directions:

1. Preheat your wood pellet grill to high and close the lid for 15 minutes.
2. Sprinkle both sides of steaks with the garlic salt, salt, and pepper and add them to the grill.
3. Grill for 5 minutes per side and spread the steaks with the mustard.
4. Sprinkle with the Parmesan cheese and minced garlic and grill for another 2 minutes.
5. Let rest for at least 5 minutes before serving.

Roasted Prime Rib with Herbs Garlic

Preparation and Cooking Time: 5 hours and 40 minutes

Serving Size: 8

Ingredients:

- 6 lb. prime rib roast (boneless)
- 2 tablespoons red wine vinegar
- 5 cloves garlic, chopped
- 1 tablespoon rosemary, chopped
- ½ cup parsley, chopped
- ½ cup olive oil
- Prime rib rub
- 4 cups beef stock, divided
- Salt and pepper to taste

Directions:

1. Tie the rib roast with butcher's wine and add the red wine vinegar, garlic, rosemary, and parsley to a food processor.
2. Stir in the olive oil and pulse for a few more seconds, until fully blended.
3. Add the rib roast to a large plastic bag and pour the vinegar mixture into the bag.
4. Turn to coat evenly and marinate in the refrigerator for 2 hours.

5. After 2 hours, take the rib roast out of the refrigerator and season the rib roast with the prime rib rub.

6. Place the rib roast in a roasting pan and pour the beef broth into the pan.

7. Preheat your wood pellet grill to 400 degrees F and close the lid for 15 minutes.

8. Place the pan over the grill and cook for 30 minutes.

9. Reduce temperature to 225 degrees F and cook for 3 hours.

Rosemary Roast Beef

Preparation and Cooking Time: 1 hour and 40 minutes

Serving Size: 8

Ingredients:

- 8 lb. rib-eye roast, sliced into 2
- 4 tablespoons olive oil, divided
- ½ cup garlic, minced
- 3 sprigs rosemary, chopped
- 3 sprigs thyme, chopped
- 4 tablespoons peppercorns, crushed
- ½ cup smoked salt

Directions:

1. Set your wood pellet grill to smoke and reheat for 10 minutes with the lid open.
2. Set grill to high and add 3 tablespoons olive oil to a roasting pan.
3. Place it on the grill, add the roast to the pan, and sear on both sides until golden.
4. Transfer to a plate and let cool. In a bowl, combine the garlic, rosemary, thyme, peppercorns, smoked salt, and remaining olive oil and rub the roast with this mixture.

5. Cook the roast on the grill for 30 minutes on high, reduce heat to 300 degrees F and cook for another 40 minutes.

6. Let rest for 15 to 20 minutes before slicing and serving.

Peppercorn Steak with Mushroom Sauce

Preparation and Cooking Time: 3 hours and 30 minutes

Serving Size: 4

Ingredients:

- 2 cloves garlic, minced
- ½ cup Dijon mustard
- 1 tablespoon Worcestershire sauce
- 2 tablespoons bourbon
- 4 beef tenderloin steaks
- Salt to taste
- 1 tablespoon tri-color peppercorns
- 1 tablespoon olive oil
- 1 onion, diced
- 1 clove garlic, minced
- ½ cup chicken broth
- ½ cup white wine
- 16 oz. Cremini mushrooms, sliced
- ½ cup heavy cream
- Salt and pepper to taste

Directions:

1. Combine the garlic, mustard, Worcestershire sauce, and bourbon in a bowl and place the steaks on top of foil sheets.

2. Spread both sides with the mustard mixture and wrap with the foil.
3. Marinate at room temperature for 1 hour, unwrap the foil and sprinkle both sides of the steaks with the salt and peppercorns.
4. Preheat your wood pellet grill to 180 degrees F and close the lid for 15 minutes.
5. Grill the steaks for 1 hour and transfer the steaks to a plate.
6. Increase temperature to high and close the lid for another 15 minutes.
7. Put the steaks back to the grill and cook for another 30 minutes.
8. Add the olive oil to a pan over medium heat and cook the onions and garlic for 2 minutes.
9. Add the mushrooms and pour in the broth and wine. Let it simmer for 5 minutes.
10. Reduce heat to low and pour in the cream.
11. Season with salt and pepper and let the steak rest for 10 minutes before slicing.
12. 25. Pour the sauce over the steak slices and serve.

Barbecue Steaks

Preparation and Cooking Time: 3 hours

Serving Size: 4

Ingredients:

- 32 oz. tomahawk rib-eye
- ¼ cup dry barbecue rub
- Salt to taste
- 3 tablespoons butter

Directions:

1. Rub the steaks with the salt and let sit at room temperature for 1 hour.
2. Close the lid for 15 minutes and sprinkle both sides of the steak with the dry barbecue rub.
3. Let sit for 15 minutes and add the steaks to the grill.
4. Cook for 45 minutes and let rest for 10 minutes.
5. Put a cast-iron pan on the grill and increase temperate to 500 degrees F.
6. Once the pan is very hot, sear the steak on the pan for 1 minute per side and transfer it to a plate.
7. Top with the butter and let rest for 10 minutes before serving.

Beef Chili

Preparation and Cooking Time: 2 hours and 15 minutes

Serving Size: 8

Ingredients:

- 1 lb. lean ground beef
- 1 lb. ground chorizo
- 2 tablespoons butter
- 1 onion, chopped
- 1 red bell pepper, chopped
- 1 green bell pepper, chopped
- 2 cloves garlic, minced
- 15 oz. canned tomato sauce
- 2 tablespoons tomato paste
- 15 oz. canned stewed tomatoes
- 30 oz. canned ranch-style beans
- 3 tablespoons cumin
- 2 bay leaves
- 3 tablespoons chili powder
- 3 tablespoons Mexican oregano
- Salt to taste

Directions:

1. Preheat your wood pellet grill to 350 degrees F and close the lid for 15 minutes.

2. In a Dutch oven over medium heat, cook the ground beef and chorizo until browned and drain the fat.

3. Add the butter and cook onion and bell peppers for 10 minutes, stir in the garlic and cook for 2 minutes.

4. Pour in the tomato sauce, tomato paste, stewed tomatoes, and beans and bring to a boil.

5. Add the cumin, bay leaves, chili powder, oregano, and salt and reduce heat and simmer for 10 minutes.

6. Transfer the Dutch oven to the grill and cook for 1 hour.

Paprika Steak

Preparation and Cooking Time: 1 hour and 40 minutes

Serving Size: 4

Ingredients:

- ½ tablespoon onion powder
- 1 tablespoon paprika
- Salt and pepper to taste
- ½ tablespoon garlic powder
- 1 teaspoon ground mustard
- ½ tablespoon brown sugar
- ¼ teaspoon cayenne pepper
- 2 tomahawk steaks

Directions:

1. Combine the paprika, garlic powder, mustard, brown sugar, onion powder, cayenne pepper, salt, and pepper in a bowl and sprinkle both sides of the steaks with this mixture.
2. Preheat your wood pellet grill to 225 degrees F and close the lid for 15 minutes.
3. Grill the steaks for 1 hour and increase the temperature to 450 degrees F.
4. Cook the steaks for 10 minutes per side.
5. Let steaks rest for 5 to 10 minutes before serving.

Pellet Grill Meatloaf

Preparation Time: 30 minutes

Cooking Time: 6 Hours

Servings: 8

Ingredients:

- 1 cup breadcrumbs
- 2 pounds ground beef
- ¼ pound ground sausage
- 2 large eggs (beaten)
- 2 garlic cloves (grated)
- ½ teaspoon ground black pepper
- ¼ teaspoon red pepper flakes
- ½ teaspoon salt or to taste
- 1 teaspoon dried parsley
- 1 green onion (chopped)
- 1 teaspoon paprika
- ½ teaspoon Italian seasoning
- 1 small onion (chopped)
- 1 cup milk
- 1 cup BBQ sauce
- ½ cup apple juice

Directions:

1. Preheat the grill to 225°F with the lid closed for 15 minutes, using apple pellet

2. In a large mixing bowl, combine the egg, milk, parsley, onion, green onion, paprika, Italian seasoning, breadcrumbs, ground beef, ground sausage, salt, pepper flakes, black pepper, and garlic. Mix thoroughly until the ingredients are well combined.

3. Form the mixture into a loaf, wrap the loaf loosely in tin foil and use a knife to poke some holes in the foil. The holes will allow the smoke flavor to enter the loaf.

4. Place the wrapped loaf on the grill grate and grill for 1 hour 30 minutes.

5. Meanwhile, combine the BBQ sauce and apple juice in a mixing bowl.

6. Tear off the top half of the tin foil to apply the glaze. Apply the glaze over the meatloaf. Continue grilling until the internal temperature of the meatloaf is 160°F.

7. Remove the meatloaf from the grill and let it sit for a few minutes to cool.

8. Cut and serve.

BBQ Brisket

Preparation Time: 30 minutes

Cooking Time: 6 Hours

Servings: 8

Ingredients:

- 1 (12-14) packer beef brisket
- 1 teaspoon cayenne pepper
- 1 teaspoon cumin
- 2 tablespoons paprika
- 1 tablespoon smoked paprika
- 1 tablespoon onion powder
- 1 /2 tablespoon maple sugar
- 2 teaspoons ground black pepper
- 2 teaspoons kosher salt

Directions:

1. Combine all the ingredients except the brisket in a mixing bowl.
2. Season all sides of the brisket with the seasoning mixture as needed and wrap it in a plastic wrap. Refrigerate for 12 hours or more.
3. Unwrap the brisket and let it sit for about 2 hours or until the brisket is at room temperature.
4. Preheat the pellet grill to 225°F with lid close, using mesquite or oak wood pellet.

5. Place the brisket on the grill grate and grill for about 6 hours. Remove the brisket from the grill and wrap with foil.

6. Return brisket to the grill and cook for about 4 hours or until the brisket's temperature reaches 204°F.

7. Remove the brisket from the grill and let it sit for about 40 minutes to cool.

8. Unwrap the brisket and cut it into slices.

Tri-tip Roast

Preparation Time: 30 minutes

Cooking Time: 50 minutes

Servings: 8

Ingredients:

- 2 pounds tri-tip roast (silver skin and the fat cap removed)
- 1 teaspoon salt
- 1 teaspoon ground black pepper
- ½ teaspoon paprika
- 1 teaspoon fresh rosemary
- 1 teaspoon garlic powder
- 1 tablespoon olive oil

Directions:

1. Combine salt, pepper, garlic, paprika, and rosemary.
2. Brush the tri-tip generously with olive oil. Season the roast with seasoning mixture generously.
3. Preheat the grill smoker 225°F with the lid closed for 15 minutes, using hickory, mesquite, or oak wood pellet.
4. Place the tri-tip roast on the grill grate directly and cook for about 1 hour or until the tri tip's temperature reaches 135°F.

5. Remove the tri-tip from the grill and wrap it with heavy-duty foil. Set aside in a cooler.

6. Adjust the grill temperature to high and preheat with lid closed for 15 minutes.

7. Remove the tri-tip from the foil, place it on the grill, cook for 8 minutes, and turn the tri-tip after the first 4 minutes.

8. Remove the tri-tip from the grill and let it rest for a few minutes to cool.

9. Cut them into slices against the grain and serve.

Baby Back Rib

Preparation Time: 30 minutes

Cooking Time: 5 hours

Servings: 8

Ingredients:

- ½ cup BBQ sauce
- 1 rack baby back ribs
- 1 cup apple cider
- 1 tablespoon Worcestershire sauce
- 1 teaspoon paprika
- ½ cup packed dark brown sugar
- 2 tablespoons yellow mustard
- 2 tablespoon honey
- 2 tablespoon BBQ rub

Directions:

1. Remove the membrane on the back of the rib with a butter knife.
2. Combine the mustard, paprika, ½ cup apple cider, and Worcestershire sauce.
3. Rub the mixture over the rib and season the rib with BBQ rub.
4. Start your grill on the smoke setting and leave the lid opened until the fire starts.

5. Close the lid and preheat the grill to 180°F using a hickory wood pellet.

6. Place the rib on the grill, smoke side up --smoke for 3 hours.

7. Remove the ribs from the grill.

8. Tear off two large pieces of heavy-duty aluminum foil and place one on a large working surface. Place the rib on the foil, rib side up.

9. Sprinkle the sugar over the rib. Top it with honey and the remaining apple cider.

10. Place the other piece of foil over the rib and crimp the aluminum foil pieces' edges together to form an airtight seal.

11. Place the sealed rib on the grill and cook for 2 hours.

12. After the cooking cycle, gently remove the foil from the rib and discard it.

13. Brush all sides of the baby back rib with the BBQ sauce.

14. Return the rib to the grill grate directly and cook for an additional 30 minutes or until the sauce coating is firm and thick.

15. Remove the rib from the grill and let it cool for a few minutes.

16. Cut into sizes and serve.

Delicious Soy Marinated Steak

Preparation Time: 20 minutes

Cooking Time: 55 minutes

Servings: 4

Ingredients:

- 1/2 chopped onion
- 3 chopped cloves of garlic
- 1/4 cup of olive oil
- 1/4 cup of balsamic vinegar
- 1/4 cup of soy sauce
- 1 tablespoon of Dijon mustard
- 1 tablespoon of rosemary
- 1 teaspoon of salt to taste
- 1/2 teaspoon of ground black pepper to taste
- 1 1/2 pounds of flank steak

Directions:

1. Using a large mixing bowl, add all the ingredients on the list aside from the steak, then mix properly to combine.
2. Place the steak in a Ziploc bag, pour in the prepared marinade then shake properly to coat.
3. Place the bag in the refrigerator and let the steak marinate for about thirty minutes to two full days.

4. Preheat the Wood Pellet Smoker and Grill to 350-400ºF, remove the steak from its marinade, then set the marinade aside for blasting.

5. Place the steak on the preheated grill, then grill for about six to eight minutes until the beef is heated through.

6. Flip the steak over and cook for an additional six minutes until an inserted thermometer reads 150ºF.

7. Place the steak on a cutting board and let rest for

Grilled Steak and Vegetable Kebabs

Preparation Time: 15 minutes

Cooking Time: 20 minutes

Servings: 5

Ingredients:

Marinade

- 1/4 cup of olive oil
- 1/4 cup of soy sauce
- 1 1/2 tablespoons of fresh lemon juice
- 1 1/2 tablespoons of red wine vinegar
- 2 1/2 tablespoons of Worcestershire sauce
- 1 tablespoon of honey
- 2 teaspoons of Dijon mustard
- 1 tablespoon of garlic
- 1 teaspoon of freshly ground black pepper to taste

Kebabs

- 1 3/4 lbs. of sirloin steak
- 1 sliced zucchini.
- 3 sliced bell peppers
- 1 large and sliced red onion
- 1 tablespoon of olive oil
- Salt and freshly ground black pepper to taste
- 1/2 teaspoon of garlic powder

Directions:

1. Using a large mixing bowl, add in the oil, soy sauce, lemon juice, red wine vinegar, Worcestershire sauce, Dijon, honey, garlic, and pepper to taste, then mix properly to combine.

2. Use a sharp knife, cut the steak into smaller pieces or cubes, and then add to a resealable bag.

3. Pour the marinade into the bag with steak, then shake to coat. Let the steak marinate for about three to six hours in the refrigerator.

4. Preheat the Wood Pellet Smoker and Grill to 425ºF, place the veggies into a mixing bowl, add in oil, garlic powder, salt, and pepper to taste, then mix to combine.

5. Thread the veggies and steak alternately unto skewers, place the skewers on the preheated grill, and grill for about eight to nine minutes until it is cooked through.

6. Make sure you turn the kebabs occasionally as you cook. Serve.

Grilled Coffee Rub Brisket

Preparation Time: 30 minutes

Cooking Time: 15 hours

Servings: 4

Ingredients:

- 1 (14 pounds) whole brisket
- Coffee Rub
- 2 tablespoons of coarse salt to taste
- 2 tablespoons of instant coffee
- 2 tablespoons of garlic powder
- 2 tablespoons of smoked paprika
- 1 tablespoon of pepper to taste
- 1 tablespoon of crushed coriander
- 1 tablespoon of onion powder
- 1 teaspoon of chili powder
- 1/2 teaspoon of cayenne

Directions:

1. Using a large mixing bowl, add in the instant coffee, garlic powder, paprika, coriander, onion powder, chili powder, cayenne, salt, and pepper to taste then mix properly to combine.

2. Rub the brisket with the prepared rub, coating all sides then set aside.

3. Preheat a Wood Pellet Smoker and Grill to 225ºF, add in the seasoned brisket, cover the smoker, and smoke for about eight hours until a thermometer reads 165ºFor the briskets.

4. Place the brisket in an aluminum foil then wrap up. Place the foil-wrapped brisket on the wood Pellet smoker and cook for another five to eight hours until the meat reaches an internal temperature of 225ºF.

5. Once cooked, let the brisket rest on the cutting board for about one hour, slice against the grain then serve.

Grilled Herb Steak

Preparation Time: 15 minutes

Cooking Time: 20 minutes

Servings: 4

Ingredients:

- 1 tablespoon of peppercorns
- 1 teaspoon of fennel seeds
- 3 large and minced cloves of garlic
- 2 teaspoons of kosher salt to taste
- 1 tablespoon of chopped rosemary
- 1 tablespoon of chopped thyme
- 2 teaspoons of black pepper to taste
- 2 teaspoons of olive oil
- 1 pound of flank steak

Directions:

1. Using a grinder or a food processor, add in the peppercorns and the fennel seeds then blend until completely crushed then add to a mixing bowl.

2. Add in the garlic, rosemary, thyme, salt, and pepper to taste then mix properly to combine, set aside.

3. Rub the steak with oil, coating all sides then coat with half of the peppercorn mixture. Make sure the steak is coated all round.

4. Place the steak in a Ziploc plastic bag then let marinate in the refrigerator for about 2 to 8 minutes.

5. Preheat a Wood Pellet Smoker and Grill to 450ºF, place the coated steak on the grill and cook for about five to six minutes.

6. Flip the steak over and cook for another five to six minutes until cooked through.

7. Once cooked, let the steak cool for a few minutes, slice, and serve.

Cocoa Rub Steak

Preparation Time: 20 minutes

Cooking Time: 40 minutes

Servings: 4

Ingredients:

- 4 ribeye steaks
- 2 tablespoons of unsweetened cocoa powder
- 1 tablespoon of dark brown sugar
- 1 tablespoon of smoked paprika
- 1 teaspoon of sea salt to taste
- 1 teaspoon of black pepper
- 1/2 teaspoon of garlic powder
- 1/2 teaspoon of onion powder

Directions:

1. Using a large mixing bowl, add in the cocoa powder, brown sugar, paprika, garlic powder, onion powder, and salt to taste, then mix properly to combine

2. Rub the steak with about two tablespoons of the spice mixture, coating all sides, then let rest for a few minutes.

3. Preheat the Wood Pellet Smoker and Grill to 450°F, place the steak on the grill, and grill for a

few minutes on both sides until it is cooked as desired.

4. Once cooked, cover the steak in foil and let rest for a few minutes serve and enjoy.

Beef Tenderloin

Preparation Time: 10 minutes

Cooking Time: 1 hour 20 minutes

Servings: 12

Ingredients:

- 1 (5-pound) beef tenderloin, trimmed
- Kosher salt, as required
- ¼ cup olive oil
- Freshly ground black pepper, as required

Directions:

1. With kitchen strings, tie the tenderloin at 7-8 places.
2. Season tenderloin with kosher salt generously.
3. With a plastic wrap, cover the tenderloin and keep aside at room temperature for about 1 hour.
4. Preheat the Z Grills Wood Pellet Grill & Smoker on grill setting to 225-250ºF.
5. Coat tenderloin with oil evenly and season with black pepper.
6. Arrange tenderloin onto the grill and cook for about 55-65 minutes.
7. Place cooking grate directly over hot coals and sear tenderloin for about 2 minutes per side.

8. Remove the tenderloin from the grill and place onto a cutting board for about 10-15 minutes before serving.

9. With a sharp knife, cut the tenderloin into desired-sized slices and serve.

Mustard Beef Short Ribs

Preparation Time: 15 minutes

Cooking Time: 3 hours

Servings: 6

Ingredients:

For Mustard Sauce:

- 1 cup prepared yellow mustard
- 1/4 cup red wine vinegar
- 1/4 cup dill pickle juice
- 2 tablespoons soy sauce
- 2 tablespoons Worcestershire sauce
- 1 teaspoon ground ginger
- 1 teaspoon granulated garlic

For Spice Rub:

- 2 tablespoons salt
- 2 tablespoons freshly ground black pepper
- 1 tablespoon white cane sugar
- 1 tablespoon granulated garlic

For Ribs:

- 6 (14-ounce) (4-5-inch long) beef short ribs

Directions:

1. Preheat the Z Grills Wood Pellet Grill & Smoker on smoke setting to 230-250ºF, using charcoal.
2. In a bowl, mix all ingredients.

3. Coat the ribs with sauce generously and then sprinkle with spice rub evenly.

4. Place the ribs onto the grill over indirect heat, bone side down. Cook for about 1-1½ hours.

5. Flip the side and cook for about 45 minutes. Repeat.

6. Remove the ribs from the grill and place onto a cutting board for about 10 minutes before serving.

7. With a sharp knife, cut the ribs into equal-sized individual pieces and serve.

Mesmerizing Beef Jerky

Preparation Time: 15 minutes

Cooking Time: 12 hours 15 minutes

Servings: 12

Ingredients:

- 2 cups of teriyaki sauce
- 1 cup of soy sauce
- 1 cup of brown sugar
- 1 dash of Worcestershire sauce
- ¼ pound fresh pineapple, peeled and sliced
- 2 cloves of garlic
- 2 pound of ground beef cut up into ½ inch thick strips

Directions:

1. Take a large-sized bowl and add teriyaki sauce, brown sugar, soy sauce, and Worcestershire sauce
2. Add garlic and pineapple to a food processor and process until smooth
3. Pour the pineapple mixture into the sauce mix and stir; transfer the whole mix to a resealable bag. Transfer the beef to the bag as well and coat it thoroughly, squeeze out as much air as possible, and zip the bag

4. Store in your fridge and allow it to marinate for 6-8 hours

5. Take your drip pan and add water; cover with aluminum foil. Preheat your Smoker to 225 degrees F

6. Use water fill water pan halfway through and place it over drip pan. Add wood chips to the side tray

7. Drain the beet from the marinade and transfer to your Smoker

8. Smoke for 6-8 hours until the jerky is chewy but not crispy. Serve and enjoy!

Original Beef Meatballs

Preparation Time: 30 minutes

Cooking Time: 2 hours

Servings: 10

Ingredients:

- 1 pound of ground beef
- ½ a pound of ground bacon
- 1 pound of pork
- 3 ounce of asiago cheese, grated
- ½ of red bell pepper, chopped
- ¼ of a large yellow onion, chopped
- 3 garlic cloves
- 1/3 cup of breadcrumbs
- 2 whole eggs
- 1/2 a cup of rub
- BBQ Sauce of your favorite brand
- For rub
- 2 teaspoons of salt
- 1 teaspoon of basil
- 1 teaspoon of sage
- 1 teaspoon of oregano
- ½ a teaspoon of thyme
- 1 and a ½ teaspoon of garlic powder
- 1 teaspoon of dill

- 1 teaspoon of marjoram
- 1 teaspoon of cornstarch
- 1 teaspoon of pepper
- 1 teaspoon of dried parsley flakes
- 1 teaspoon of rosemary
- ½ a teaspoon of ground cinnamon
- ½ a teaspoon of ground nutmeg

Directions:

1. For making the rub, add all of the listed (rub) ingredients into a blender and blend them well to a fine powder
2. Clear up your blender and add your roughly chopped onion, bell pepper, and garlic to your food processor
3. Pulse it well until it is nicely pureed
4. Add all of the ingredients into a bowl of a stand mixer
5. Using a paddle attachment, mix everything for about 1 minute at medium settings
6. Once the mixture is nicely tacky, it is ready
7. Take your drip pan and add water; cover with aluminum foil. Preheat your Smoker to 225 degrees F

8. Use water fill water pan halfway through and place it over drip pan. Add wood chips to the side tray

9. Using the meat mixture, form them into as many balls as possible

10. Use Frogrmats if possible and place them on top of the grate

11. Place your meatballs and smoke them for about 1 or 1 and a half hour until the internal temperature reaches 165 degrees Fahrenheit. Once done, transfer them to a pan and toss them in the BBQ sauce

Smoked Up Bulgogi

Preparation Time: 15 minutes

Cooking Time: 16 hours + 30 minutes

Serving: 8-10

Ingredients:

- 5 pound of Chuck Roast
- Every day yellow mustard
- Foil pan

For Rub

- 1 tablespoon of salt
- 2 teaspoons of black pepper
- 1 teaspoon of cayenne pepper
- 1 teaspoon of oregano
- ½ a teaspoon of chili powder
- 2 teaspoons of garlic powder

For Bulgogi

- 2 pound (or more) of shaved chuck roast beef
- 4 cloves of garlic
- 1 inch of ginger
- 1 teaspoon of chili flakes
- 3 tablespoon of Korean hot sauce
- 4 tablespoon of red wine vinegar
- 6 tablespoon of soy sauce
- 6 tablespoon of sesame oil

Vegetables

- 1 green pepper
- 1 medium-sized onion
- 2 carrots
- Oil as needed

Directions:

1. Rinse meat thoroughly under cold water
2. Apply a nice coating of yellow mustard over the meat
3. Take a small bowl and mix all the ingredients listed under the rub
4. Sprinkle/massage the rub all over the sides of your meat
5. Take your drip pan and add water; cover with aluminum foil. Preheat your Smoker to 235 degrees F
6. Use water fill water pan halfway through and place it over drip pan. Add wood chips to the side tray
7. Gently place your meat onto the smoker grate
8. Smoke them for about 8-12 hours until the thickest part of the beef gives an internal temperature of 195 degrees Fahrenheit
9. Once the temperature is reached, wrap it up and let it rest for about 1 hour

10.   It is now ready to be used for the Bulgogi

11.   Slice up about 2-3 pound of meat off your chuck roast

12.   Take a food processor and add garlic and ginger; process them until a fine paste forms

13.   Take a bowl and add pepper flakes, garlic/ginger paste, brown sugar, Korean hot sauce, rice wine vinegar, sesame oil, and soy sauce

14.   Mix them well to prepare the marinade

15.   Take a hot pan and add the beef slices alongside the marinade and simmer them until fully cooked

16.   Take another pan and add butter

17.   Add the vegetables and stir fry them to brown them

18.   If you are serving in a burger bun, then take your bread and place a layer of cheese

19.   Add the meat followed by the vegetables, according to your preference

20.   Let it rest for about 2 minutes and serve!

Gourmet Beef Jerky

Preparation Time: 8-10 hours

Cooking Time: 6-8 hours

Servings: 6

Ingredients:

- 2 cups of soy sauce
- 1 cup of Worcestershire sauce
- 1 cup of cranberry grape juice
- 1 cup of teriyaki sauce
- 1 tablespoon of hot pepper sauce
- 2 tablespoon of steak sauce
- 1 cup of light brown sugar
- ½ a teaspoon of ground black pepper
- 2 pound of flank steak, cut up into ¼ inch slices

Directions:

1. Take a bowl and whisk in soy sauce, cranberry grape juice, teriyaki sauce, Worcestershire sauce, steak sauce, brown sugar, hot sauce, and black pepper

2. Mix well and pour the mixture into a resealable bag

3. Add flank steak to the bag and coat with the marinade

4. Squeeze as much air as possible and seal. Allow it to refrigerate for 8-10 hours

5. Remove the steak from the marinade and wipe any excess

6. Take your drip pan and add water, cover with aluminum foil. Preheat your Smoker to 225 degrees F

7. Use water fill water pan halfway through and place it over drip pan. Add wood chips to the side tray and transfer the steak to your middle rack of the Smoker and Smoker for 6-8 hours, making sure to keep adding more chips after every 1 hour. Serve and enjoy!

Smoked Mustard Beef Ribs

Preparation Time: 25 minutes

Cooking Time: 4 to 6 hours

Servings: 4 to 8

Ingredients:

- 2 (2- or 3-pound / 907- or 1360-g) racks beef ribs
- 2 tablespoons yellow mustard
- 1 batch sweet and spicy cinnamon rub

Directions:

1. Preheat the grill, with the lid closed, to 225ºF (107ºC).

2. Remove the membrane from the backside of the ribs. This can be done by cutting just through the membrane in an X pattern and working a paper towel between the membrane and the ribs to pull it off.

3. Coat the ribs all over with mustard and season them with the rub. Using your hands, work the rub into the meat.

4. Place the ribs directly on the grill grate and smoke until their internal temperature reaches between 190°F (88°C) and 200°F (93ºC).

5. Remove the racks from the grill and cut them into individual ribs. Serve immediately.

Braised Beef Short Ribs

Preparation Time: 25 minutes

Cooking Time: 4 hours

Servings: 2 to 4

Ingredients:

- 4 beef short ribs, Salt, to taste
- Freshly ground black pepper, to taste
- ½ cup beef broth

Directions:

1. Preheat the grill, with the lid closed, to 180ºF (82ºC).

2. Season the ribs on both sides with salt and pepper.

3. Place the ribs directly on the grill grate and smoke for 3 hours.

4. Pull the ribs from the grill and place them on enough aluminum foil to wrap them completely.

5. Increase the grill's temperature to 375ºF (191ºC).

6. Fold in three sides of the foil around the ribs and add the beef broth. Fold in the last side, completely enclosing the ribs and liquid. Return the wrapped ribs to the grill and cook for 45 minutes more. Remove the short ribs from the grill, unwrap them, and serve immediately.

Smoked Pastrami

Preparation Time: 15 minutes

Cooking Time: 12 to 16 hours

Servings: 6 to 8

Ingredients:

- 1 (8-pound / 3.6-kg) corned beef brisket
- 2 tablespoons yellow mustard
- 1 batch Espresso Brisket Rub
- Worcestershire Mop and Spritz, for spritzing

Directions:

1. Preheat the grill, with the lid closed, to 225°F (107°C).

2. Coat the brisket all over with mustard and season it with the rub. Using your hands, work the rub into the meat. Pour the mop into a spray bottle.

3. Place the brisket directly on the grill grate and smoke until its internal temperature reaches 195°F (91°C), spritzing it every hour with the mop.

4. Pull the corned beef brisket from the grill and wrap it completely in aluminum foil or butcher paper. Place the wrapped brisket in a cooler, cover the cooler, and let it rest for 1 or 2 hours.

5. Remove the corned beef from the cooler and unwrap it. Slice the corned beef and serve.

Sweet & Spicy Beef Brisket

Preparation Time: 10 minutes

Cooking Time: 7 hours

Servings: 10

Ingredients:

- 1 cup paprika
- ¾ cup sugar
- 3 tablespoons garlic salt
- 3 tablespoons onion powder
- 1 tablespoon celery salt
- 1 tablespoon lemon pepper
- 1 tablespoon ground black pepper
- 1 teaspoon cayenne pepper
- 1 teaspoon mustard powder
- ½ teaspoon dried thyme, crushed
- 1 (5-6-pound) beef brisket, trimmed

Directions:

1. In a bowl, place all ingredients except for beef brisket and mix well.
2. Rub the brisket with spice mixture generously.
3. With a plastic wrap, cover the brisket and refrigerate overnight.
4. Preheat the Z Grills Wood Pellet Grill & Smoker on grill setting to 250 degrees F.

5. Place the brisket onto grill over indirect heat and cook for about 3-3½ hours.

6. Flip and cook for about 3-3½ hours more.

7. Remove the brisket from grill and place onto a cutting board for about 10-15 minutes before slicing.

8. With a sharp knife, cut the brisket in desired sized slices and serve.

Beef Rump Roast

Preparation Time: 10 minutes

Cooking Time: 6 hours

Servings: 8

Ingredients:

- 1 teaspoon smoked paprika
- 1 teaspoon cayenne pepper
- 1 teaspoon onion powder
- 1 teaspoon garlic powder
- Salt and ground black pepper, as required
- 3 pounds beef rump roast
- ¼ cup Worcestershire sauce

Directions:

1. Preheat the Z Grills Wood Pellet Grill & Smoker on smoke setting to 200 degrees F, using charcoal.
2. In a bowl, mix together all spices.
3. Coat the rump roast with Worcestershire sauce evenly and then, rub with spice mixture generously.
4. Place the rump roast onto the grill and cook for about 5-6 hours.
5. Remove the roast from the grill and place onto a cutting board for about 10-15 minutes before serving.

6. With a sharp knife, cut the roast into desired-sized slices and serve.

Herbed Prime Rib Roast

Preparation Time: 10 minutes

Cooking Time: 3 hours 50 minutes

Servings: 10

Ingredients:

- 1 (5-pound) prime rib roast
- Salt, as required
- 5 tablespoons olive oil
- 2 teaspoons dried thyme, crushed
- 2 teaspoons dried rosemary, crushed
- 2 teaspoons garlic powder
- 1 teaspoon onion powder
- 1 teaspoon paprika
- ½ teaspoon cayenne pepper
- Ground black pepper, as required

Directions:

1. Season the roast with salt generously.
2. With a plastic wrap, cover the roast and refrigerate for about 24 hours.
3. In a bowl, mix together remaining ingredients and set aside for about 1 hour.
4. Rub the roast with oil mixture from both sides evenly.

5. Arrange the roast in a large baking sheet and refrigerate for about 6-12 hours.

6. Preheat the Z Grills Wood Pellet Grill & Smoker on smoke setting to 225-230 degrees F, using pecan wood chips.

7. Place the roast onto the grill and cook for about 3-3½ hours.

8. Meanwhile, preheat the oven to 500 degrees F.

9. Remove the roast from grill and place onto a large baking sheet.

10. Place the baking sheet in oven and roast for about 15-20 minutes.

11. Remove the roast from oven and place onto a cutting board for about 10-15 minutes before serving.

12. With a sharp knife, cut the roast into desired-sized slices and serve.

BBQ Spiced Flank Steak

Preparation Time: 15 minutes

Cooking Time: 30 minutes

Servings: 6

Ingredients:

- 1 (2-pound) beef flank steak
- 2 tablespoons olive oil ¼ cup BBQ rub
- 3 tablespoons blue cheese, crumbled
- 2 tablespoons butter, softened
- 1 teaspoon fresh chives, minced

Directions:

1. Preheat the Z Grills Wood Pellet Grill & Smoker on grill setting to 225 degrees F.
2. Coat the steak with oil evenly and season with BBQ rub. Place the steak onto the grill and cook for about 10-15 minutes per side.
3. Remove the steak from grill and place onto a cutting board for about 10 minutes before slicing.
4. Meanwhile, in a bowl, add blue cheese, butter and chives and mix well.
5. With a sharp knife, cut the steak into thin strips across the grain.
6. Top with cheese mixture and serve.

Beef Stuffed Bell Peppers

Preparation Time: 20 minutes

Cooking Time: 1 hour

Servings: 6

Ingredients:

- 6 large bell peppers
- 1 pound ground beef
- 1 small onion, chopped
- 2 garlic cloves, minced
- 2 cups cooked rice
- 1 cup frozen corn, thawed
- 1 cup cooked black beans
- 2/3 cup salsa
- 2 tablespoons Cajun rub
- 1½ cups Monterey Jack cheese, grated

Directions:

1. Cut each bell pepper in half lengthwise through the stem.
2. Carefully, remove the seeds and ribs.
3. For stuffing: heat a large frying pan and cook the beef for about 6-7 minutes or until browned completely.
4. Add onion and garlic and cook for about 2-3 minutes.

5. Stir in remaining ingredients except cheese and cook for about 5 minutes.

6. Remove from the heat and set aside to cool slightly.

7. Preheat the Z Grills Wood Pellet Grill & Smoker on grill setting to 350 degrees F.

8. Stuff each bell pepper half with stuffing mixture evenly.

9. Arrange the peppers onto grill, stuffing side up and cook for about 40 minutes.

10. Sprinkle each bell pepper half with cheese and cook for about 5 minutes more.

11. Remove the bell peppers from grill and serve hot.

BBQ Meatloaf

Preparation Time: 20 minutes

Cooking Time: 2½ hours

Servings: 8

Ingredients:

For Meatloaf:

- 3 pounds ground beef
- 3 eggs
- ½ cup panko breadcrumbs
- 1 (10-ounce) can diced tomatoes with green chile peppers
- 1 large white onion, chopped
- 2 hot banana peppers, chopped
- 2 tablespoons seasoned salt
- 2 teaspoons liquid smoke flavoring
- 2 teaspoons smoked paprika
- 1 teaspoons onion salt
- 1 teaspoons garlic salt
- Salt and ground black pepper, as required

For Sauce:

- ½ cup ketchup
- ¼ cup tomato-based chile sauce
- ¼ cup white sugar
- 2 teaspoons Worcestershire sauce

- 2 teaspoons hot pepper sauce
- 1 teaspoon red pepper flakes, crushed
- 1 teaspoon red chili pepper
- Salt and ground black pepper, as required

Directions:

1. Preheat the Z Grills Wood Pellet Grill & Smoker on smoke setting to 225 degrees F, using charcoal.
2. Grease a loaf pan.
3. For meatloaf: in a bowl, add all ingredients and with your hands, mix until well combined.
4. Place the mixture into prepared loaf pan evenly.
5. Place the pan onto the grill and cook for about 2 hours.
6. For sauce: in a bowl, add all ingredients and beat until well combined.
7. Remove the pan from grill and drain excess grease from meatloaf.
8. Place sauce over meatloaf evenly and place the pan onto the grill.
9. Cook for about 30 minutes.
10. Remove the meatloaf from grill and set aside for about 10 minutes before serving.
11. Carefully, invert the meatloaf onto a platter.
12. Cut the meatloaf into desired-sized slices and serve.

Smoked Beef Brisket in Sweet and Spicy Rub

Preparation Time: 15 minutes

Cooking Time: 1 hour

Servings: 10

Ingredients:

- Beef Brisket (6-lbs., 2.7-kgs)
- 1 cup paprika
- ½ cup salt
- 1 cup brown sugar
- ½ cup cumin
- ½ cup pepper
- ½ cup chili powder ¼ cup cayenne pepper

Directions:

1. Combine paprika, salt, brown sugar, cumin, pepper, chili powder, and cayenne pepper in a bowl then stir until incorporated.
2. Rub the beef brisket with the spice mixture then marinate overnight. Store in the refrigerator to keep it fresh.
3. Remove the beef brisket from the refrigerator then thaw until it reaches room temperature.

4. Preheat the smoker to 250°F (121°C) with charcoal and hickory chips—using indirect heat. Don't forget to soak the wood chips before using.

5. When the smoker has reached the desired temperature, wrap the beef brisket with aluminum foil then place it in the smoker.

6. Smoke the wrapped beef brisket for 8 hours. Check the temperature every hour then adds more charcoal and hickory chips if it is necessary.

7. Once the smoked beef brisket is ready, remove from the smoker then let it sit for a few minutes until warm.

8. Unwrap the smoked beef brisket then place on a flat surface.

9. Cut the smoked beef brisket into thick slices then place on a serving dish.

10. Serve and enjoy.

Simple Smoked Beef Brisket with Mocha Sauce

Preparation Time: 15 minutes

Cooking Time: 1 hour

Servings: 10

Ingredients:

- 5 pounds beef brisket
- 1 ½ tablespoons garlic powder
- 1 ½ tablespoons onion powder
- 4 tablespoons salt
- 4 tablespoons pepper
- 2 ½ tablespoons olive oil
- 1 cup chopped onion
- 2 teaspoons salt
- ¼ cup chopped chocolate dark
- ¼ cup sugar –
- ½ cup beer –
- 2 shots espresso

Directions:

1. Rub the beef brisket with garlic powder, onion powder, salt, and black pepper.
2. Wrap the seasoned beef brisket with a sheet of plastic wrap then store in the refrigerator overnight.

3. In the morning, remove the beef brisket from the refrigerator and thaw for about an hour.

4. Preheat the smoker to 250°F (121°C) with charcoal and hickory chips—using indirect heat. Place the beef brisket in the smoker and smoke for 8 hours.

5. Keep the temperature remain at 250°F (121°C) and add some more charcoal and hickory chips if it is necessary.

6. Meanwhile, preheat a saucepan over medium heat then pour olive oil into the saucepan.

7. Once the oil is hot, stir in chopped onion then sauté until wilted and aromatic.

8. Reduce the heat to low then add the remaining sauce ingredients to the saucepan. Mix well then bring to a simmer.

9. Remove the sauce from heat then set aside.

10. When the smoked beef brisket is ready, or the internal temperature has reached 190°F (88°C), remove from the smoker then transfer to a serving dish.

11. Drizzle the mocha sauce over the smoked beef brisket then serve.

12. Enjoy warm.

Lemon Ginger Smoked Beef Ribs

Preparation Time: 10 minutes

Cooking Time: 10 hours

Servings: 10

Ingredients:

- 6 pounds beef ribs
- 3 tablespoons paprika
- ¼ cup brown sugar
- 1 ½ tablespoons dry mustard
- 1 ½ tablespoons ginger
- 1 tablespoon onion powder
- 1 ½ tablespoons salt
- 1 tablespoon pepper
- 3 tablespoons lemon juice

Directions:

1. Combine paprika with brown sugar, dry mustard, onion powder, salt, and pepper then mix well.
2. Rub the beef ribs with the spice mixture then place on a sheet of aluminum foil.
3. Splash lemon juice over the beef ribs then sprinkle ginger on top.
4. Wrap the seasoned beef ribs with the aluminum foil then set aside.

5. Preheat the smoker to 250°F (121°C) with charcoal and hickory chips—don't forget to soak the wood chips before using.

6. Place the wrapped beef ribs in the smoker and smoke for 10 hours.

7. Check the temperature remain at 250°F (121°C) and add some more charcoal and hickory chips if it is necessary.

8. Once the smoked beef ribs are done, remove from the smoker.

9. Unwrap the smoked beef ribs then place on a serving dish.

10.   Serve and enjoy.

Chocolate Smoked Beef Ribs

Preparation Time: 15 minutes

Cooking Time: 19 hours

Servings: 10

Ingredients:

- 6 pounds beef ribs
- 1 ¼ cups cocoa powder
- ¾ cup chili powder
- ¾ cup sugar
- ¾ cup salt
- ¼ cup black pepper
- ¼ cup cumin

Directions:

1. Place the cocoa powder in a bowl then add chili powder, sugar, salt, black pepper, and cumin in the bowl. Mix well.
2. Rub the beef ribs with the cocoa powder mixture then cover with plastic wrap.
3. Marinate the beef ribs overnight and store in the refrigerator to keep it fresh.
4. In the morning, remove the beef ribs from the refrigerator and thaw for about an hour.
5. Preheat the smoker to 250°F (121°C) with charcoal and hickory chips—using indirect heat.

Place the beef ribs in the smoker and smoke for 10 hours.

6. Keep the temperature remain at 250°F (121°C) and add some more charcoal and hickory chips if it is necessary.

7. Once it is done or the internal temperature has reached 170°F (77°C), take the smoked beef ribs out from the smoker and transfer to a serving dish.

8. Serve and enjoy warm.

Smoked and Pulled Beef

Preparation Time: 10 minutes

Cooking Time: 6 hours

Servings: 6

Ingredients:

- 4 lb. beef sirloin tip roast
- 1/2 cup BBQ rubs
- 2 bottles of amber beer
- 1 bottle barbecues sauce

Directions:

1. Turn your wood pellet grill onto smoke setting then trim excess fat from the steak.

2. Coat the steak with BBQ rub and let it smoke on the grill for 1 hour.

3. Continue cooking and flipping the steak for the next 3 hours. Transfer the steak to a braising vessel that adds the beers.

4. Braise the beef until tender, then transfer to a platter reserving 2 cups of cooking liquid.

5. Use a pair of forks to shred the beef and return it to the pan. Add the reserved liquid and barbecue sauce. Stir well and keep warm before serving. Enjoy.

Smoked Midnight Brisket

Preparation Time: 15 minutes

Cooking Time: 12 hours

Servings: 6

Ingredients:

- 1 tbsp. Worcestershire sauce
- 1 tbsp. Pellet beef Rub
- 1 tbsp. Pellet Chicken rubs
- 1 tbsp. Pellet Blackened Saskatchewan rub
- 5 lb. flat cut brisket
- 1 cup beef broth

Directions:

1. Rub the sauce and rubs in a mixing bowl then rub the mixture on the meat.
2. Preheat your grill to 180°F with the lid closed for 15 minutes. You can use super smoke if you desire.
3. Place the meat on the grill and grill for 6 hours or until the internal temperature reaches 160°F.
4. Remove the meat from the grill and double wrap it with foil.
5. Add beef broth and return to grill, with the temperature increased to 225°F. Cook for 4 hours or until the internal temperature reaches 204°F.

6. Remove from grill and let rest for 30 minutes.
   Serve and enjoy with your favorite BBQ sauce.

Grilled Butter Basted Porterhouse Steak

Preparation Time: 15 minutes

Cooking Time: 40 minutes

Servings: 4

Ingredients:

- 4 tbsp. butter, melted
- 2 tbsp. Worcestershire sauce
- 2 tbsp. Dijon mustard
- Pellet Prime rib rub

Directions:

1. Set your wood pellet grill to 225°F with the lid closed for 15 minutes.
2. In a mixing bowl, mix butter, sauce, Dijon mustard until smooth. Brush the mixture on the meat then season with the rub.
3. Arrange the meat on the grill grate and cook for 30 minutes.
4. Use tongs to transfer the meat to a patter then increase the heat to high.
5. Return the meat to the grill grate to grill until your desired doneness is achieved.
6. Baste with the butter mixture again if you desire and let rest for 3 minutes before serving. Enjoy.

Cocoa Crusted Grilled Flank Steak

Preparation Time: 15 minutes

Cooking Time: 6 minutes

Servings: 7

Ingredients:

- 1 tbsp. cocoa powder.
- 2 tbsp. chili powder
- 1 tbsp. chipotle chili powder
- 1/2 tbsp. garlic powder
- 1/2 tbsp. onion powder
- 1-1/2 tbsp. brown sugar
- 1 tbsp. cumin
- 1 tbsp. smoked paprika
- 1 tbsp. kosher salt
- 1/2 tbsp. black pepper
- Olive oil
- 4 lb. Flank steak

Directions:

1. Whisk together cocoa, chili powder, garlic powder, onion powder, sugar, cumin, paprika, salt, and pepper in a mixing bowl.
2. Drizzle the steak with oil then rub with the cocoa mixture on both sides.

3. Preheat your wood pellet grill for 15 minutes with the lid closed.

4. Cook the meat on the grill grate for 5 minutes or until the internal temperature reaches 135°F.

5. Remove the meat from the grill and let it cool for 15 minutes to allow the juices to redistribute.

6. Slice the meat against the grain and on a sharp diagonal.

7. Serve and enjoy.

Wood Pellet Grill Prime Rib Roast

Preparation Time: 5 minutes

Cooking Time: 4 hours

Servings: 10

Ingredients:

- 7 lb. bone prime rib roast
- Pellet prime rib rub

Directions:

1. Coat the roast generously with the rub then wrap in a plastic wrap. Let sit in the fridge for 24 hours to marinate.

2. Set the temperatures to 500°F.to to preheat with the lid closed for 15 minutes.

3. Place the rib directly on the grill fat side up and cook for 30 minutes.

4. Reduce the temperature to 300°F and cook for 4 hours or until the internal temperature is 120°F-rare, 130°F-medium rare, 140°F-medium and 150°F-well done.

5. Remove from the grill and let rest for 30 minutes, then serve and enjoy.

Smoked Longhorn Cowboy Tri-Tip

Preparation Time: 15 minutes

Cooking Time: 4 hours

Servings: 7

Ingredients:

- 3 lb. tri-tip roast
- 1/8 cup coffee, ground
- 1/4 cup Pellet beef rub

Directions:

1. Preheat the grill to 180°F with the lid closed for 15 minutes.

2. Meanwhile, rub the roast with coffee and beef rub. Place the roast on the grill grate and smoke for 3 hours.

3. Remove the roast from the grill and double wrap it with foil. Increase the temperature to 275°F.

4. Return the meat to the grill and let cook for 90 minutes or until the internal temperature reaches 135°F.

5. Remove from the grill, unwrap it and let rest for 10 minutes before serving.

6. Enjoy.

Wood Pellet Grill Teriyaki Beef Jerky

Preparation Time: 15 minutes

Cooking Time: 5 hours

Servings: 10

Ingredients:

- 3 cups soy sauce
- 2 cups brown sugar
- 3 garlic cloves
- 2-inch ginger knob, peeled and chopped
- 1 tbsp. sesame oil
- 4 lb. beef, skirt steak

Directions:

1. Place all the ingredients except the meat in a food processor. Pulse until well mixed.
2. Trim any excess fat from the meat and slice into ¼ inch slices. Add the steak with the marinade into a zip lock bag and let marinate for 12-24 hours in a fridge.
3. Set the wood pellet grill to smoke and let preheat for 5 minutes.
4. Arrange the steaks on the grill, leaving a space between each. Let smoke for 5 hours.
5. Remove the steak from grill and serve when warm.

Grilled Butter Basted Rib-Eye

Preparation Time: 20 minutes

Cooking Time: 20 minutes

Servings: 4

Ingredients:

- 2 rib-eye steaks, bone-in
- Salt to taste
- Pepper to taste
- 4 tbsp. butter, unsalted

Directions:

1. Mix steak, salt, and pepper in a Ziplock bag. Seal the bag and mix until the beef is well coated. Ensure you get as much air as possible from the Ziplock bag.

2. Set the wood pellet grill temperature to high with closed lid for 15 minutes. Place a cast-iron into the grill.

3. Place the steaks on the hottest spot of the grill and cook for 5 minutes with the lid closed.

4. Open the lid and add butter to the skillet when it's almost melted place the steak on the skillet with the grilled side up.

5. Cook for 5 minutes while busting the meat with butter. Close the lid and cook until the internal temperature is 130°F.

6. Remove the steak from skillet and let rest for 10 minutes before enjoying with the reserved butter.

Smoked Beef with Smoked Garlic Mayo Dip

Preparation Time: 15 minutes

Cooking Time: 8 hours

Servings: 10

Ingredients:

- 5 pounds beef tenderloin
- ¼ cup minced garlic
- 2 teaspoons black pepper
- 2 teaspoons salt
- 1 ½ teaspoons olive oil
- 5 cloves garlic
- ½ cup mayonnaise
- ¼ cup water
- 2 tablespoons red wine vinegar
- 2 tablespoons chives

Directions:

1. Preheat the smoker to 250°F (121°C). Soak the hickory wood chips for about an hour before using.
2. Combine minced garlic, black pepper, salt, and olive oil then stir until mixed.
3. Rub the beef tenderloin with the spice mixture then place in the smoker.

4. Wrap the garlic cloves with aluminum foil then place next to the beef tenderloin.

5. Smoke the beef tenderloin and garlic for about 8 hours or until the internal temperature of the beef tenderloin reaches 145°F (63°C).

6. Remove the smoked beef tenderloin and garlic from the smoker then cut the smoked beef tenderloin into slices. Set aside.

7. Place mayonnaise and chives in a blender then pour water and red wine vinegar over mayonnaise.

8. Add the smoked garlic to the blender then blend until smooth.

9. Transfer the garlic and mayonnaise dip to a small bowl then place next to the smoked beef tenderloin.

10.   Serve and enjoy.

Simple Smoked Pulled Beef

Preparation Time: 15 minutes

Cooking Time: 9 hours

Servings: 10

Ingredients:

- 1 6-pound chuck roast
- 2 ½ tablespoons salt
- 2 ½ tablespoons black pepper
- 2 ½ tablespoons garlic powder
- ½ cup chopped onion
- 3 cups beef broth

Directions:

1. Preheat the smoker to 225°F (107°C). Let the lid closed and wait for 15 minutes.
2. Mix garlic powder with black pepper and salt until combined.
3. Rub the chuck roast with the spice mixture then using your hand massage the roast until it is thoroughly seasoned.
4. Place the seasoned roast on the grill then cook the roast for 3 hours. Spray the roast with beef broth once every hour.

5. After 3 hours, sprinkle chopped onion on the bottom of a pan then pours the remaining beef broth over the onion—about 2 cups.

6. Transfer the cooked roast to the pan then place the pan on the grill.

7. Increase the smoker's temperature to 250°F (121°C) then cooks for 3 hours more.

8. After 3 hours, cover the pan with aluminum foil then lower the temperature to 165°F (74°C).

9. Cook the roast for another 3 hours until done.

10.   Once it is done, transfer the smoked beef to a flat surface and let it cool.

11.   Once it is cold, using a fork shred the beef then place on a serving dish.

12.   Serve and enjoy!

Spiced Smoked Beef with Oregano

Preparation Time: 10 minutes

Cooking Time: 8 hours

Servings: 10

Ingredients:

- 1 8-pounduntrimmed brisket
- 6 tablespoons paprika
- ¼ cup salt
- 3 tablespoons garlic powder
- 2 tablespoons onion powder
- 1 ½ tablespoons black pepper
- 1 ½ tablespoons dried parsley
- 2 ½ teaspoons cayenne pepper
- 2 ½ teaspoons cumin
- 1 ½ teaspoons coriander
- 2 teaspoons oregano
- ½ teaspoon hot chili powder
- Preheat the smoker prior to smoking.
- Add woodchips during the smoking time.

Directions:

1. Cook the brisket for 6 hours.
2. After 6 hours, usually the smoker temperature decreases to 170°F (77°C).
3. Take the brisket out from the smoker then wrap with aluminum foil.

4. Return the brisket to the smoker then cooks again for 2 hours—this will increase the tenderness of the smoked beef.
5. Once it is done, remove the smoked beef from the smoker then place in a serving dish.
6. Cut the smoked beef into slices then enjoy!

BBQ Sweet Pepper Meatloaf

Preparation Time: 20 minutes

Cooking Time: 3 hours and 15 minutes

Servings: 8

Ingredients:

- 1 cup chopped red sweet peppers
- 5 pounds ground beef
- 1 cup chopped green onion
- 1 tablespoon salt
- 1 tablespoon ground black pepper
- 1 cup panko breadcrumbs
- 2 tablespoon BBQ rub and more as needed
- 1 cup ketchup
- 2 eggs

Directions:

1. Switch on the Pellet grill, fill the grill hopper with Texas beef blend flavored wood pellets, power the grill on by using the control panel, select 'smoke' on the temperature dial, or set the temperature to 225 degrees F and let it preheat for a minimum of 5 minutes.

2. Meanwhile, take a large bowl, place all the ingredients in it except for ketchup and then stir until well combined.

3. Shape the mixture into meatloaf and then sprinkle with some BBQ rub.

4. When the grill has preheated, open the lid, place meatloaf on the grill grate, shut the grill, and smoke for 2 hours and 15 minutes.

5. Then change the smoking temperature to 375 degrees F, insert a food thermometer into the meatloaf and cook for 45 minutes or more until the internal temperature of meatloaf reaches 155 degrees F.

6. Brush the top of meatloaf with ketchup and then continue cooking for 15 minutes until glazed.

7. When done, transfer food to a dish, let it rest for 10 minutes, then cut it into slices and serve.

Blackened Steak

Preparation Time: 10 minutes

Cooking Time: 60 minutes

Servings: 4

Ingredients:

- 2 steaks, each about 40 ounces
- 4 tablespoons blackened rub
- 4 tablespoons butter, unsalted

Directions:

1. Switch on the Pellet grill, fill the grill hopper with hickory flavored wood pellets, power the grill on by using the control panel, select 'smoke' on the temperature dial, or set the temperature to 225 degrees F and let it preheat for a minimum of 15 minutes.

2. Transfer steaks to a dish and then repeat with the remaining steak.

3. Let seared steaks rest for 10 minutes, then slice each steak across the grain and serve.

Thai Beef Skewers

Preparation Time: 15 minutes

Cooking Time: 8 minutes

Servings: 6

Ingredients:

- ½ of medium red bell pepper, destemmed, cored, cut into a ¼-inch piece
- ½ of beef sirloin, fat trimmed
- ½ cup salted peanuts, roasted, chopped
- 1 teaspoon minced garlic
- 1 tablespoon grated ginger
- 1 lime, juiced
- 1 teaspoon ground black pepper
- 1 tablespoon sugar
- 1/4 cup soy sauce
- 1/4 cup olive oil

Directions:

1. Prepare the marinade and for this, take a small bowl, place all of its ingredients in it, whisk until combined, and then pour it into a large plastic bag.
2. Cut into beef sirloin 1-1/4-inch dice, add to the plastic bag containing marinade, seal the bag, turn it upside down to coat beef pieces with the

marinade and let it marinate for a minimum of 2 hours in the refrigerator.

3. When ready to cook, switch on the Pellet grill, fill the grill hopper with cherry flavored wood pellets, power the grill on by using the control panel, select 'smoke' on the temperature dial, or set the temperature to 425 degrees F and let it preheat for a minimum of 5 minutes.

4. Meanwhile, remove beef pieces from the marinade and then thread onto skewers.

5. When the grill has preheated, open the lid, place prepared skewers on the grill grate, shut the grill, and smoke for 4 minutes per side until done.

6. When done, transfer skewers to a dish, sprinkle with peanuts and red pepper, and then serve.

Lightning Source UK Ltd.
Milton Keynes UK
UKHW020640180621
385739UK00011B/618

9 781803 300498